Concord

by Laurie Rozakis
illustrated by Ben Fine

Chapters

Orlando   Boston   Dallas   Chicago   San Diego

Visit *The Learning Site!*

www.harcourtschool.com

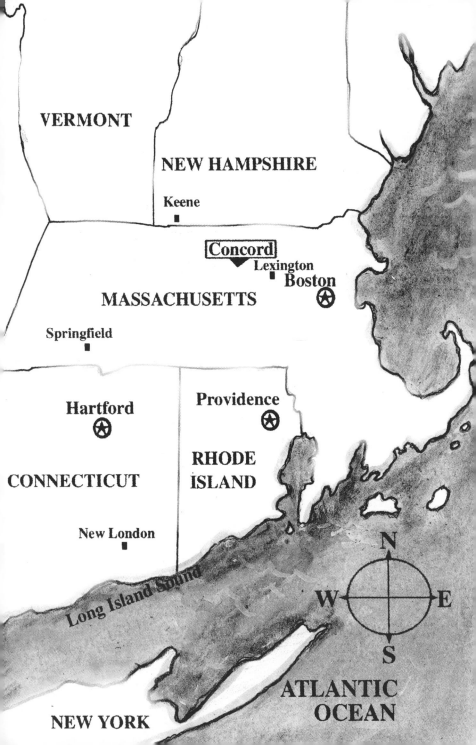

Concord, Long Ago

The town of Concord is in the state of Massachusetts. The English who settled there named the town Concord in 1635. The town is located on the Concord River. The river made it a wonderful location for a town. The river flows to the Atlantic Ocean. As you will read, Native Americans lived in the area long before the English came.

Let's go back in time to visit the area. For thousands of years, the area was home to Native Americans. They called the area "Musketaquid."

Why was this area a good place for people to settle? An important reason was the river. The river was filled with fish, which could provide food for people. People could travel on the river. It was a good way to move things from place to place.

By around 1000 B.C., the Algonquian people lived there. The Algonquians were a group of Native American tribes. The tribes shared the same language. They shared the same customs.

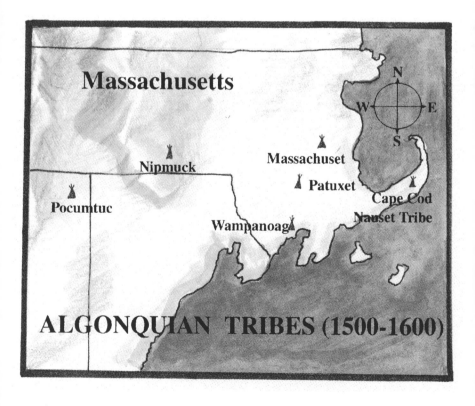

ALGONQUIAN TRIBES (1500-1600)

The woods were filled with animals to hunt. There were deer, beavers, raccoons, bears, opossums, geese, and wild turkeys. The Algonquians cooked their meat on sticks over an open fire. They did not use a pot or an iron skillet.

On the broad fields, Algonquian women farmed corn, beans, squashes, and pumpkins. They sprinkled their crops with water from the river. Women and children gathered wild grapes, picked nuts from the trees, and dug clams.

Algonquian women owned the tribe's land. They were important members of the society. Family trees and other information about the different tribes show this. They show that families were traced according to who their mothers and grandmothers were. When a young Algonquian man married, he joined his bride's family.

The tribes did not move camp often. They usually went back and forth between two places. They would move according to the seasons and where they were able to get food.

The woods were thick with big trees. Some measured 30 feet around! To clear the land, Algonquians cut the bark all the way around each tree. This killed the tree. When it fell, it could easily be cut into wood for fires.

After making firewood, the men burned the branches and leaves. The ash was worked into the soil. It made the soil better for farming. In this way, Algonquians made open fields with rich soil for growing crops.

The river was filled with many fish. To catch them, the Algonquians set up small dams, or weirs, in the Concord River. They built these small traps with twigs and mud. People often gathered at the fishing weirs to catch fish, talk with each other, and help each other with their traps.

In the spring, there were plenty of fish. The Algonquians had fun playing games and holding contests at the fishing weirs. They had a good time while gathering lots of food.

Along the river, the Algonquians built one-
room houses from thin branches lashed together
with vines. The houses were covered with bark.
Each house had a curved roof covered with strong
reeds. This type of house is called a wigwam.

In the open areas, the children turned
cartwheels and played ball games. It would be fun
to stay and watch their games, but we have to fly
through time to the 1600s.

Colonial Concord

In the early 1600s, many English settlers had come to Musketaquid. In 1635, the English asked the Algonquians for some land. The Algonquians made a peaceful agreement with the English and gave them the land. The English named the town that they built on the land "Concord." *Concord* means "peace and harmony."

The English farmed the rich land and fished the clear waters of the Concord River. Concord was not a boomtown. There were no gold nuggets and no miners. There was "peace and harmony." However, it didn't even last 150 years.

10

In 1763, America was a colony of Great Britain, not an independent country. To pay off the colony's debts, Great Britain made American colonists pay very heavy taxes on goods brought in from Britain. There were taxes on stamps required on publications and legal documents, tea, paper, and many everyday items. Americans thought such high taxes were very unfair.

For these reasons and others, Americans decided it was time to break away from Great Britain to become an independent country.

Lexington and Concord

In April 1775, the British learned that the colonists had gathered a large supply of gunpowder in Concord. The British set out to capture some of the rebels and take the gunpowder. They would go through the town of Lexington and on to Concord. Luckily for the Americans, a silversmith named Paul Revere learned of the British plan. He and other patriots had been spying on the British. Revere made a plan of his own. With two other men, William Dawes and Dr. Samuel Prescott, he decided to warn the patriots.

Revere, Dawes, and Prescott knew that the British were coming. They just did not know how the British would come. Revere suggested that a warning system be set up. If the British were coming by land, one lighted lantern would be hung in a Boston church tower. If they were coming by sea, two lanterns would be hung there.

The three men could not risk traveling by stagecoach, so they rode horses. On the night of April 18, 1775, they rode to Lexington. They warned, "The British are coming! The British are coming!"

Early in the morning on April 19, the British soldiers arrived by land in Lexington. The minutemen, as they were called, were ready for them.

The leader of the American soldiers said, "Stand your ground. Don't fire unless fired upon. But if they mean to have a war, let it begin here!"

The British leader ordered the Americans to leave. A shot was fired. The Battle of Lexington began. It was the start of the American Revolution.

Then the British went on to Concord. There, too, the minutemen were ready for them. The gunpowder was hidden in farmhouses, barns, and fields. The British only found some of it. Minutemen gathered at the North Bridge by the Concord River. Other colonists came to join them.

After several people were wounded, the British soldiers retreated. They went back to Boston. It was a great victory for the Americans.

In 1837, Ralph Waldo Emerson wrote the "Concord Hymn." It was written for the opening of the Concord Monument. The Concord Monument is a landmark that stands where the British and Americans fought. In his hymn, Emerson called the first shot of the American Revolution, "the shot heard round the world."

Today, when visitors go to Concord they can see the Concord Monument and a minuteman statue. Both help people remember that important day in American history.